Behind Media

Television

Catherine Chambers

Heinemann Library
Chicago, Illinois

Designed by Paul Davies and Associates
Originated by Ambassador Litho Ltd.
Printed in Hong Kong, China

05 04 03 02 01
10 9 8 7 6 5 4 3 2 1

Library of Congress Cataloging-in-Publication Data
Chambers, Catherine, 1966-
  Television / Catherine Chambers.
    p. cm. -- (Behind media)
  Includes bibliographical references and index.
  ISBN 1-58810-035-9
  1. Television broadcasting--Juvenile literature. [1. Television broadcasting.] I. Title. II.
Series.

  PN1992.57 .C49 2001
  384.55--dc21

                                        00-046166

Acknowledgments
The author and publishers are grateful to the following for permission to reproduce copyright material: Arena, pp. 9, 16, 27, 29; Big Pictures, p. 45; Trevor Clifford, reprinted with permission from TV Guide Magazine Group, Inc., publisher of *TV Guide* magazine©, p. 6; Corbis, p. 43; Jacques M. Chenet, p. 22; Rick Rappaport, p. 15; Fulvio Roiter, p. 36; Ronald Grant, pp. 7, 10, 14; The Kobal Collection, p. 8; Moviestore Collection, p. 13; NASA/Science Photo Library, p. 38; PA Photos/Neil Munns, p. 5; Pearson Television, pp. 4, 23, 24, 26, 32; Polygram/The Kobal Collection, p. 12; Science Photo Library/Vaughan Fleming, p. 41; Sony, p. 31; Stay Still/Caroline Mardon, p. 28; The Stock Market/Tom Stewart, p. 21; Tony Stone Images, p. 35; Walter Hodges, p. 19; Greg Pease, pp. 25, 34; Michael Rosenfeld, p. 42; Tek Image/Science Photo Library, p. 39.

Cover photograph reproduced with permission of Pearson Television.

Our thanks to Des Lyver for his comments in the preparation of this book.

Every effort has been made to contact copyright holders of any material reproduced in this book. Any omissions will be rectified in subsequent printings if notice is given to the publisher.

Some words are shown in bold, **like this.** You can find out what they mean by looking in the glossary.

Contents

The TV Phenomenon

Introduction. 4
A World of Television 6

Creating Comedy

What's the Situation? 8
What's the Big Idea? 10
Winning Ways 12

Getting It off the Ground

Paying the Piper 14
The Starting Block 16
Writing It Down 18

Be Prepared

Acting It Out 20
Comical Characters 22
Practice Makes Perfect 24
Setting the Scene 26

The Real Thing

Let's Roll! 28
Lights, Camera, Action! 30
How Does It Sound? 32
From Camera to Control Room 34

Behind the Screen

Invisible Waves 36
New Ways for Waves 38
Light Fantastic 40

The End of the Show

Taking a Break 42
The Verdict and Future Trends 44
Glossary 46
Index 48

The TV Phenomenon

Introduction

Over 70 years ago, when radio and film were just entering their golden age, a new electronic mass communication system was being developed—television. Not only could people listen to it in their own homes, they could also watch it. It was another twenty years before television really got off the ground, but then it quickly became a source of education and information, relaxation and entertainment. This book takes you through TV's financing and organization, its production processes and people, and its **ratings** and rewards, concentrating especially on the production of TV's most popular **genre**—the sitcom.

What is the big attraction?

You can watch television all day and all night. You can sit in front of a two-hour movie or flip through a choice of dozens of channels **transmitting** everything from discussion to dance. A TV screen can be so small that you can hold it in your hand, while a TV projector can pan the picture as wide as a wall. It is no wonder that with such variety, around 80 percent of the U.S. population owns a television set, while in the U.K. and Australia there is one TV for every two people. We will find out what makes people watch television in later chapters.

The set is a huge illusion. Even many of the props are designed for visual effect and do not actually work. Behind the scenes, a creative and practical team makes sure that the television audience sees the set as reality. Lighting and camera work complete the illusion.

Who makes it happen?

Sitcom stars are always making the headlines. Behind the glamour and the rumors, though, there lies a whole team of creative and technical personnel, from the **director** and **floor manager** to the head of **props** and the stage hand. We will look at the roles and challenges of those working on the set of a television show and in the **control room.** We will also explore the requirements of the sitcom genre in terms of acting and production techniques.

What's next?

Beginning in the 1960s, the video recorder enabled us to see our favorite TV programs again and again. Cable, satellite, and now **digital** TV have expanded the number of channels available to us, so that in large countries such as the U.S. several thousand stations are able to broadcast, both locally and nationally. Digital television has also improved the quality of both sound and reception. We will find out more about the technical developments in television.

Will it last?

"Video killed the radio star." This line from a pop song sums up how, from the 1950s, television eclipsed radio as the most popular mass communication medium. Perhaps something could eclipse television in the future. For now, however, it appears TV is here to stay.

Who invented television?

There really is no single person to credit with the invention of television. It was a combination of the efforts of different scientists and was a truly international affair. It included a Scottish amateur scientist, John Logie Baird, an American engineer, Philo T. Farnsworth, and a Russian-American physicist, Vladimir Zworykin. Color television, developed in the 1950s, was widely broadcast in the 1960s and on.

Television personalities are now at least as famous as film stars, and many sitcom actors move to the big screen. Television awards ceremonies bring out the glitz and the glamour of the industry—but there is a downside. Like film stars, television sitcom and soap opera stars, such as the members of the cast of Friends seen here, have problems with privacy from both the media and obsessive fans.

A World of Television

A well-known American media analyst, Anthony Smith, once said, "The way a country organizes its broadcasting system reveals a strange, coded version of that country's entire political culture." It is true that throughout the world, television mirrors ideologies, economies, and tastes.

The way it is run

Every country organizes its broadcasting according to its financial and political structure and its basic beliefs. In many countries, freedom of expression has led to a huge diversity in programming, catering to every interest imaginable. This is especially true in the U.S., where there are several mainstream **network** television companies—NBC, ABC, CBS, and Fox—as well as many independents and several thousand satellite and cable services.

The stars and the stories are discussed at length in numerous newspaper columns, magazines, and behind-the-scenes books. Having an article published in one of these publications is one of the main ways to advertise a TV show. They also show how each TV station fights for publicity for its sitcoms, hoping to increase ratings.

Censorship

In the Communist-run Soviet Union, many households owned a television set by the 1950s, but stations were state-run, programs were tightly controlled, and news was censored. The situation is still similar in China, although it is changing as the country opens up more to the world. With satellite TV and the Internet, it is increasingly difficult to deny people access to information and entertainment.

In the U.S., the industry's regulatory body is the Federal Communications Commission (FCC), which allocates licenses and **wavebands.** It also enforces the industry's regulations, including technical details, such as standards of color quality **transmission,** but the FCC is not entitled to censor program content. It relies largely on the industry to regulate itself.

Most other countries operate a national network, such as the Australian Broadcasting Company (ABC) and the British Broadcasting Company (BBC), both of which transmit throughout their respective nations. Independent commercial companies operate, too, to provide diversity and competition. Some countries dedicate a channel to a particular purpose, such as France's Channel 5, which transmits education and information programs. Similar to this is the U.S.'s Public Broadcasting Service (PBS), which gives us *Sesame Street.*

Our shrinking earth

In many ways, television has made the world a smaller place. Through the small screen, we are made aware of cultures, conflicts, and discoveries far from our own homes. We are allowed into the amazing, secret world of creatures and their natural habitats, often totally removed from anything on our own doorstep. On a more mundane level, television trends also ripple around the world, as programs are **dubbed** or subtitled and sold abroad. Also, television companies carefully study the **ratings** of overseas successes and then try to copy the successful shows.

*Game shows and sitcoms are two of the most popular television **genres** in most countries. For almost 50 years they have attracted investment and enabled television to expand into other areas.*

The U.S., with its hundreds of channels, is the largest market for English-speaking television programs and films, but it is also one of the greatest exporters, particularly of sitcoms and, in recent years, documentaries about natural disasters and ecological issues. Game shows, too, have crossed oceans—notably the highly successful *Who Wants to be a Millionaire?* Ideas are also borrowed, as well as complete productions. These are adapted to suit different cultural climates. Again, sitcom ideas and characters have traveled and translated well. One of the most controversial has been the 1960s–1970s U.K. role of Alf Garnett in *Till Death Us Do Part,* mirrored in the 1970s by the equally startling U.S. character, Archie Bunker.

Creating Comedy

What's the Situation?

The sitcom—or situation comedy—explores the reactions of people and the relationships between them in specific situations. Through different types of humor, from **slapstick** and silly to scathing and cynical, audiences have come to relish observing the quirky aspects of everyday life.

The big attraction

What is so appealing about watching people struggle through different situations in their lives? For this is really what most sitcoms are about. Many feature the characters' inability to resolve practical problems or to sort out relationships. Unlike us, they manage to bumble through it all in a humorous way, and even if the characters are not always happy about their lot, the way they show their misery makes us smile, often with a sense of recognition. It is this identification with characters and situations that makes the sitcom so successful.

In the last fifteen years, the most successful sitcoms have come out of the U.S. and have been bought by television companies throughout the world. What makes the sitcom so easily appreciated by other cultures? Unlike stand-up comedy, the successful universal sitcom does not rely for its popularity only on jokes, one-liners, and puns that are often **culture-specific** and **language-specific.** A sitcom, even for its own home audience, builds its appeal on situations and emotions that everyone can recognize.

The earliest form of the TV sitcom first hit the screens in the 1950s. It was initially a vehicle for radio comedians and media personalities. Two of the most successful sitcoms were I Love Lucy *and* Here Comes Lucy, *based on the fictional daily life of comedian Lucille Ball. These sitcoms had a theatrical tone, both in acting and in reacting to an audience.*

Following the format

A sitcom is usually constructed as a series of about six to twelve half-hour programs, each with the same main title and characters. In a series, almost every episode is a complete story. It has what is called **"closure."** Within each series there are ongoing mini-plots, which are resolved only in the last episode of each series. Some of these mini-plots involve the viewer with the trials and triumphs of each character. Others are the ongoing storylines of the situations themselves, maybe the school that a particular sitcom is based around, for instance. Only at the end of the series, or the end of the whole sitcom, will the viewer know the exact fate of the characters and the situation. These mini-plots follow the **serial format,** normally used in dramas and adaptations of novels, which comprises a strong central storyline subdivided into different episodes. Each episode has a cliffhanger ending—one that keeps the audience in suspense—rather than a neat closure.

Sitcom **producers** and writers use a variety of devices to keep people watching a whole series and maintain **ratings.** One of these devices is delay—keeping the audience in suspense about a relationship or an event until well into the series. One of the most compelling "will they, won't they?" delays was the developing relationship of Niles and Daphne in *Frasier.*

A sitcom usually takes place on one or more sets that rarely change. The situation is nearly always the same, but some scenes or whole episodes do take place on location, as seen here.

On the job

Anyone wanting to be part of a creative team needs a good grasp of English and a thorough knowledge of sitcoms—both from the home country and abroad. Members of creative teams often have a degree or certificate in media studies. Television agencies, studios, and production companies accept ideas for sitcoms as well as scripts. Many companies actually employ creative teams to think up ideas that are then sent to a scriptwriter.

What's the Big Idea?

Television companies are always on the lookout for new sitcom ideas, but there is never any guarantee of success, even if a similar idea has previously attracted big audiences. Good ideas come from various places.

Hidden gems

Many **serialized** television dramas are developed from ideas brought to the television company by individual **producers** or **directors.** Some are thrashed out by development teams, while a few are picked from the thousands sent to them by hopeful amateurs. Sitcom writers themselves often come up with new themes, too. Many of these writers are long-established TV scriptwriters and often collaborate. Some have long-standing partnerships—one writer perhaps specializing in characterization and plot, and another in one-line gags and wisecracks.

Successful scenarios

There is a certain amount of luck in creating a hit sitcom, but there is also a lot of hard work trying to find the winning formula—the unique script, the imaginative director, and the cast that gels. Producers and production companies know the psychology of attracting an audience through the sitcom. The burning question is usually what type of situation to base a series on.

In recent years, relationships between partners, brothers and sisters, parents and children, bosses and workers, and teachers and students have provided classic situations, but rarely has the scenario in which these relationships take place been the main source of comedy. Most scenarios serve only as the sitcom's background. This contrasts with earlier sitcoms in which the scenario itself threw up all sorts of chaotic and comic situations to which the characters had to react. The 1960s sitcom *Green Acres*, about a newlywed couple of city-slickers trying out the "good life" in a run-down rural homestead, and the U.K. classic, *Fawlty Towers*, set in a seedy seaside hotel, are two good examples. This last sitcom breaks away from the more usual attraction of characters and situations that we can identify with. *Fawlty Towers* is far less comfortable than most sitcoms; its situations are quite bizarre and its central character, Basil Fawlty, is totally wacky.

There are few locations that have not been tried. They range from hospitals, schools, and churches to hotels, cafés, and bars. The different types of characters have included monster *Munsters*, *Bewitched* witches, and alien visitors in *Third Rock from the Sun*. Despite all these different contexts, ordinary human nature is the main theme—and this is what we relate to. This is what we find so funny.

On the job

The sitcom script-reader's job is not easy, but if they pick a winner they will be very satisfied and well rewarded. A script-reader needs very good English skills and a thorough knowledge of TV sitcom trends. They have to be able to see ahead, making sure that a good idea will last more than one or two episodes. Many script-readers start in agencies as script-readers' assistants.

Situation, characterization, acting, and scripted humor are the main ingredients for a sitcom, but the personalities of the main characters, such as in Seinfeld, *shown here, are often what makes the sitcom a real success.*

Different audiences

Some sitcoms are based around a specific age group. *Friends* is very much a 20- to 30-something sitcom. It acts as a funny flip side to a basketful of more serious drama series based on people of a similar age. Teen sitcoms such as *Saved by the Bell*, *City Guys*, and *Sabrina, the Teenage Witch* often try to reflect the problems, anxieties, and triumphs of young people in an adult-controlled world.

Winning Ways

What makes a sitcom a winner? Humor is unpredictable, but there are certain things that will make the majority of us laugh. Most successful sitcom humor lies in the way that the characters behave and relate to each other.

Carving out characters

Characterization is one of the keys to sitcom success. Together, sitcom characters give us a rounded picture of life and relationships, but if you look at them individually you will see that most of the characters are **stereotypes.** Each sitcom character has a dominant personality trait and a clearly drawn, specific role, such as the dry wit of Chandler in *Friends* or the flawed hero "The Fonz" in *Happy Days*. The skill of writers and actors is to make us believe that these types of people exist—to make the fictitious characters seem real. Each part's exaggerated characteristic creates humor. So, too, does the contrast between these strong stereotypes.

Occasionally, in a particular episode, a character performs "out of character," that is, he or she tries to change his or her personality. This, too, is often humorous, as it nearly always lands the character in a difficult situation. By the end of the episode he or she has usually returned to normal. Many sitcom writers try to incorporate a message into each episode, and the one here is that it's best to simply be yourself.

The U.K.'s Mr. Bean *is a one-man sitcom that has traveled well, finding success in many parts of the world, including the U.S. The Mr. Bean character does not seem to be able to cope in the modern world. His painful puzzlement and innocence is both sad and funny. The character is brilliantly acted by Rowan Atkinson, who manages to create humor from his bodily and facial actions and reactions in a variety of scenarios.*

Laughing at failure

Failure can be funny. At least that is what scriptwriters seem to think, for many of the characters often fail to achieve what they want, whether in a relationship or a working situation. Characters are often made to go to great lengths in order to succeed in something. These desperate attempts are often what make us laugh.

In recent years, the most successful sitcom writers have created characters who are full of anxieties. They are always analyzing and worrying about themselves and their relationships with others. *Cheers*, *Seinfeld*, *Friends*, and *Frasier* all share in this trend. Kelsey Grammer, the lead actor in *Frasier*, has performed this type of intense personality through a variety of sitcom roles, building on his previous experience.

Does humor travel?

American sitcoms are some of the most sought-after programs. They are broadcast on **prime-time** TV in many parts of the world. Even **dubbing** and subtitling do not take anything away from the popularity of their brand of humor. Most of the countries that import American sitcoms also produce their own, and use their own **culture-specific** devices to attract audiences. However, some do contain characters and types of humor that can also be recognized in other cultures. These foreign sitcoms are successfully exported to other parts of the world, too—even to the U.S.

Slapstick humor rarely dominates a sitcom. It is used very sparingly, often to show a surprising side to a straight character. Slapstick is used to good effect in the sitcom Third Rock from the Sun, which is illustrated here. Mostly, it reinforces the ridiculous aspect of the somber, quaint chief of the aliens, Dick Solomon.

Double act

Many sitcoms have two types of characters: comical and straight. The humor of the comical character is made even funnier by the contrast it makes with the straight character, who acts as a foil for the humorous partner. Some straight roles, though, are amusing in themselves, for their glumness and their rather dull ways. They react to the comedy of a situation with an unrealistic seriousness or lack of concern.

Getting It off the Ground

Paying the Piper

Financing is the first consideration when creating a sitcom. The **executive producer** sets and runs the budget and the administration policies and processes. Sitcoms can attract some of the best television **ratings,** so a lot of money is often spent to make sure they are successful. Those working on sitcoms can command very high fees. The money to cover these costs can come from a variety of places.

Who pays?

State-owned and private television companies, independent production companies, individual **producers,** and multimedia corporations are the main financiers of television sitcoms and most other TV programs. Individual, and usually "sleeping" contributors, chip in, too. These are often celebrities of other media or wealthy business people interested in the performing arts. While they cannot contribute expertise to the production, they are justly acknowledged in the credits for their financial support, which is, of course, an investment for them, too.

A small budget for a sitcom does not necessarily bring failure. Rising Damp was a 1970s British sitcom that now has cult status in the U.K. Its sets were cheap to make and there were only four main actors. The writing, highly skilled actors, and wry humor made this sitcom a winner.

Profits from sitcoms can be huge. For those produced and broadcast on commercial television, most of these profits come from the advertising that sitcoms attract. As most TV sitcoms are produced initially for **terrestrial** television, profits also come from selling the rights to satellite and cable television companies or to foreign stations. This is how publicly-financed television companies make their money. Independent companies and individual producers sell their series to the station that offers the highest bid—whether commercial or public. This bid can be renegotiated for each series.

As well as immediate profit, there can be long-term benefits from sitcoms. New productions are a risk; many flop and most attract only small-budget commercials. But, if ratings and media attention increase, so too does interest from advertising companies. The next series of the sitcom will get a **prime-time** slot and attract lucrative brand-name advertising. Both commercial and publicly-funded television stations are able to sell foreign rights more easily, too.

Counting the cost

A popular sitcom series of six episodes can cost several million dollars to produce. Some production costs are quite low—relatively few sets are needed and they are fairly inexpensive to create compared with those of, say, drama classics. Sitcom sets are seldom altered throughout a series, although they may be updated for a follow-up. Exceptions to this are, for instance, science-fiction sitcoms, which might have a main set on a space station or in a space vehicle, and several fresh sets for different planets. Costumes and make-up for science-fiction sitcoms are also more costly than those for family, school, or office-based sitcoms. Preproduction sitcom costs often include lavish up-front payments to writers and performers. **Commissioned** writers usually receive half of their fee on contract, with a quarter on the delivery of the script, and the final quarter when the script has been accepted by the producer and **director.**

Large, profitable production companies can usually finance sitcoms without borrowing money, but smaller companies need to negotiate with banks and other lenders to finance the preproduction costs.

Stretching the budget

In February 2000, the six stars of *Friends* asked for their fee for each episode to be raised from $60,000 to $300,000—in line with the stars of the last episode of *Seinfeld*. By the first week in May, the figure had risen to $600,000. Contracts were finally sealed on May 15 for around $750,000 per star for each episode. There are always ripple effects from this kind of fee increase. Advertisers are usually charged more for slots in the show, and the survival of the particular sitcom itself can be put in jeopardy.

The Starting Block

Television stations, production companies, and sometimes individual **producers** begin by **commissioning** the sitcom script or accepting material selected by their script-reading teams. These teams sift out the best scripts or ideas from the thousands they receive from agents and writers. The next job is to find a suitable production team, either within or outside the company.

Early days

Under the **executive producer,** a producer is employed to oversee the sitcom from the preproduction stage on through production and postproduction—all within the given budget. The preproduction stage includes getting together a team, including a **director** and other important members of the production team, such as the **casting** director, the set designer, and the head of photography.

Most production companies employ staff producers and crew for regular productions, such as news broadcasts, but they have to look to freelancers for other types of programs, such as a trial or pilot sitcom series. Once a series is established, and if it is successful, a regular team of the highest-skilled production workers will be employed on staff.

Difficult decisions

The producer of a TV program is always limited during the planning stage by money, time, the number and quality of staff that can be hired, and the size of the studios and their facilities. Another consideration is whether the production is **live,** live-on-tape, or **prerecorded** and **edited.** For the sitcom, a live production means filming in front of an audience. This affects cost, studio space, and recording techniques.

Picking the slot

As with any program, scheduling the sitcom is crucial for **ratings** and depends a lot on the suitability of the content. School and "teen-angst" sitcoms are usually scheduled for late afternoon and early evening viewing, when young people are home from school, but before they go out again. *Friends* and *Frasier* have found a huge following across a wide range of ages and occupations. As many teenagers watch them, new episodes are often shown between 7:00 and 10:00 P.M., while repeats are scheduled for 6:00–7:00 P.M. Their popularity has secured them evening **prime-time** viewing, and with that, the draw of advertisers. A new sitcom by a well-known writer will also be given a prime-time evening slot, but an unknown writer is usually scheduled during off-peak viewing.

On the job

A producer needs to know about all aspects of television production, scheduling, and budgeting. He or she must be able to relate well to all members of the production team. There are courses available in TV production. Following this, many producers begin as producer's assistants, making sure that nothing runs over time and picking up on any problems during filming.

Together, the producer and director have to make sure that the script is screened to the best artistic effect and within budget. They must determine the number and type of sets and outdoor locations that are needed, and the amount and kind of cameras that will be used. The choices made can have a big effect on the end result.

Finding a name

Some titles are simple and descriptive (*The Cosby Show*), and often made up of one word referring to the central character or characters (*Seinfeld*, *Frasier*). These titles focus the audience on the stars and are reminiscent of character comedies. Others tell you the theme, for example *Friends* and *Happy Days*. Occasionally, titles are more cryptic. *Third Rock from the Sun* is a somewhat disparaging description of Earth, which instantly hints at the content: a group of superior aliens sent on an impossible mission—to find out what makes earthlings tick.

Writing It Down

The original script contains a summary of the plot and character sketches, and it sets each scene before the dialogue begins. It also gives action, stage directions, and a few basic camera instructions, just to give an idea of the viewpoint that the writer has in mind in particular circumstances. But this is still a raw script that needs to be developed further.

The right direction

Most sitcoms are written by more than one person. In the U.S. especially, they are developed by large teams of at least a dozen scriptwriters, but even this amount of talent cannot produce a perfect script the first time.

The **director** revises the script, and then often consults other members of the team for further revision, which can continue even throughout shooting. For instance, once **casting** has been completed, the casting director could have a slightly different idea about how a particular character might speak and react. There are often several revisions before the work becomes a rehearsal script. Extra columns are then added on the left side of the script to show camera action for each shot, **cuing,** and any other information that helps the visual image. This **camera script** is developed by the director, usually in collaboration with the senior cameraman and the lighting director, and is what everyone works from.

Keeping it clear

The **floor manager (FM)** draws up the running order from the camera script. The running order is a timetable of shots, with columns showing what cameras are to be used. The cameras are numbered so that the senior cameraman can cue in each camera when it is needed. There is a day/night column that instructs the lighting crew, and a cast column so that the floor manager knows who is supposed to be on set. Once rehearsals begin, further changes have to be made to the script and running order, as not all shots work out well in practice. Actors, too, sometimes make suggestions to improve dialogue and action. All this is done within a very short span of time.

A sample script

Television and film script **formats** are very similar—the layout opposite would be a suitable draft script to send to a production company. "INT" means interior, and outside locations are marked "EXT." The number 1 indicates that this is the first scene. The writer treats the set like a stage, and many of the instructions are very similar to those in a theatrical production.

Attracting new talent

Television companies are so anxious to attract new sitcom series that in 2000, the British Broadcasting Corporation (BBC) set up a talent competition for budding sitcom writers. Each entry had to provide a half-hour script including stage directions (about 6,000 to 7,000 words in all), an outline of the characters, a brief synopsis for each of the other episodes, and an indication of where the written script would fall within the series.

Tuff Love – Episode One

The setting

An underfunded and understaffed small-town police station. The set is a very simple, drab central office. The switchboard and reception area are hidden from the sergeant's desk by a crude partition.

1. INT POLICE STATION. DAY
ESTABLISHING SHOT
(P.C. CHAIN *receives phone call from member of public at switchboard*)

MEMBER OF PUBLIC
(*panicky*)
I've found a huge hole in the road.

P.C. CHAIN
I'll just put you through to Lost Property then.

(P.C. CHAIN *pretends to switch on recorded music, sings a tune into the phone, and then calls out to* SGT. TUFF)

A call to Lost Property, Sir!

SGT. TUFF
Hang on, there! I've just got to lick a few hundred more stamps to go on these Neighborhood Watch leaflets.

P.C. CHAIN
(*turns back to switchboard and speaks in high-pitched, telephone-sales voice*)

I'm sorry madam. Hello! Hello! Are you still there? Look, we're in a bit of a rush...

(*pulls out flashing lights from under the desk and switches on siren*)

When a sitcom script is submitted to a TV company the reader has to imagine many things—the situation, the characters, and the potential for a series. The writer helps the reader by including character sketches and an idea of the relationships among the main roles.

On the job

A sitcom writer needs to have a deep understanding of human nature and behavior and the quirks that make us funny. The first job is to thoroughly research the situation and develop the characteristics of the roles. The writer needs to be able to visualize how the lines will sound and how the characters will look on screen. He or she must make sure that there is enough material in the idea for at least six episodes, and characters that can sustain the storylines and humor for this amount of time.

Be Prepared

Acting It Out

The sitcom actor has one of the hardest jobs in the business. Comedy in itself is difficult to perform convincingly, but the sitcom actor also has to develop a realistic character. They also have to know how to move in front of a camera with a **live** audience in mind. First, though, they have to get the part!

Getting the part

Directors and **casting** directors have a good knowledge of established or up-and-coming skilled sitcom actors, so they can often cast the lead roles for a new sitcom without asking the actors to take part in a competitive audition. The chosen actors can, however, be asked to attend a script reading and a screen test to make sure that they sound and look right for the part. Smaller roles are auditioned. For this, all actors prepare speeches from classical and modern works, although they are often asked to simply read the sample script given to them by the casting director.

Living the part

Once the actor gets the part, but before stepping onto the set, he or she lives and breathes the part in preparation. For example, actors playing the roles of police officers would probably spend some time in a real police station. This would show them how the police and public interact in given situations and the basic workings of the station. They could even model their characters on real officers.

Such research is followed by group discussions and readings with the director and the rest of the main cast—and sometimes by one-to-one sessions between actor and director. Talking about the general aims of the writer, the motivation of the characters, and the objective of the episode in question all help the cast and crew to interpret the wishes of both writer and director. In order to improve **ratings,** a production company sometimes needs to promote a popular actor by bringing out his or her character—the readings and discussions help to set this straight with the other members of the cast.

The makers of method acting

Method acting was pioneered by the Russian actor, producer, and director Konstantin Stanislavsky (1863–1938). He developed his ideas while working in the Moscow Art Theatre. By the 1930s, method acting had found its way to the U.S., where it was adopted by the Group Theatre, but it was Elia Kazan who caused the training to become formally adopted at his New York Actors' Studio, founded in 1947. Variations of the method are now used all over the world.

The preparation for each episode of a sitcom is very short. This makes the sitcom actor's efforts to stay in character even more important. They also need enormous powers of concentration to block out anything that has disturbed them in between scenes or **takes,** which are different versions of a single shot or sequence. Most actors have been well trained for this.

Becoming someone else

In drama school, actors learn how to get under the skin of the characters they play in order to feel and behave as the character would. As well as studying people in real life who have roles or behavior similar to the characters', they try to learn as much about themselves as possible. This is so they can strip away their own personalities and instinctive reactions bit by bit. In other words, they deconstruct themselves in order to reconstruct a different character. They also have to learn to be reactive as well as active, for they have to respond to certain situations in a particular way. This approach is called "method acting," and is taught in most drama colleges.

Before landing a part in a sitcom or other production, an actor has to train hard. He or she has to learn how to be aware of, and control, the mind, voice, body, and face. Many actors practice specific breathing and physical exercises in order to develop an awareness and control of all their muscles—to learn how to move some parts without moving others.

Comical Characters

Whether it is theater, cinema, or television, most actors prepare themselves in a similar way for "getting into character." However, sitcom actors have to create a comical aspect to their role, often exaggerating and embellishing the over-riding characteristic of the part.

Sitcom skills

Acting for a television sitcom is very similar to theater acting, except that the voice does not have to be projected to the far side of a large theater. The sitcom actor has to exaggerate body gestures, facial expressions, and the **inflection** in his or her voice. They have to time their lines, their actions, and reactions perfectly; appropriate timing is the hallmark of a good comic actor. Each character develops his or her own timed responses to certain repeated situations. When it becomes a recognizable habit, it becomes funny. It establishes and continually reinforces the character.

Sitcom actors only have to remember their lines in short sequences, but for child actors, even this can be a challenge. Here, in The Cosby Show, *Bill Cosby and the* **floor manager** *are helping out young Keisha Knight Pullman.*

Acting and reacting

Staying in character means that an actor has to respond to situations in a uniform manner. When morbid, pessimistic, and unsmiling Victor Meldrew from the U.K.'s *One Foot in the Grave* steps out of bed and puts his foot on a hedgehog, he has to mutter, "Oh, dear," and carry on as normal, even though the situation is almost surreal and would certainly be very painful in real life. Any other reaction would simply not be as funny.

Sitcom actors also have to work out how they interrelate with other characters and react to them in a given situation. This means that each actor has to understand the roles of all the others. The relationships between them, and therefore the reactions, are often exaggerated. Characters' responses become hyper-tense in an argument, but loose and floppy when in a relaxed and informal situation. They are petulant when someone upsets them, delirious when made happy, and bowled over when shocked. This exaggeration is another source of comedy.

The final actor

Sitcom actors have to be continually aware of the audience, whether the show is **live** or televised. They have to pause for laughter in the right places even when it is canned **(prerecorded)** laughter **dubbed** onto the final tape. Actors have to react correctly to spontaneous laughter, too. Live audiences are unpredictable. This makes sitcoms more like the theater, although television actors also have to be aware of positioning for the cameras.

The audience is the last actor—so say many performers. For it is the reaction of the audience that stimulates the actors and dictates the manner in which they react. This is the same in the televised sitcom as it is for the theater. As Victoria Wood, writer and star of the U.K. sitcom *Dinnnerladies*, said, "The audience makes every episode different—you never know how they will react."

On a live show, if a particular character, action, or reaction gets a really good laugh or applause, then the actors can make sure they repeat and reinforce what that particular audience enjoyed.

Changing moods

The sitcom **format** is usually divided into three parts. The first is a state of equilibrium (balance), where everything is "normal." The second is a state of turmoil, where activities and relationships are disturbed, and the third is a return to equilibrium. This format shapes the players' actions and reactions. It requires flexibility to make the changes in the second part work, and then deep concentration in order to return the situation and the characters to normal.

Practice Makes Perfect

We have seen how actors prepare themselves for their parts and get to grips with the aims of the episode and the series, but this is only the beginning of televised sitcom rehearsal, which has to combine the acting and technical aspects to achieve a seamless show.

Showing the way

The first rehearsals take place on a makeshift set away from the studio. Here, the positioning of basic **props,** such as doors and sofas, gives the actors and the **director** an idea of how speech and movement will interact. On the set itself, the positions of the camera crew, props, and lighting are pre-planned for each scene and written on the **camera script,** as described on page 18. These form the framework for the actors, who are then brought onto the set for a preliminary rehearsal, or walk-through. This is a rehearsal of the basic actions and reactions without any dialogue. It shows where the actors are shadowing each other, requiring the director to redirect their action. Working out the performers' positions is known as blocking, and the walk-through is sometimes called the blocking rehearsal. The director can use this rehearsal to adjust lighting and props and assess costume and make-up. Before shooting a sitcom, some directors use the rehearse-record technique, where there is a run-through of each shot before the first **take.** Others go straight into shooting. Much depends on whether the sitcom is being filmed **live** or is **prerecorded.**

*Even the sitcom studio audience has to rehearse! The **floor manager (FM)** explains how he wants the audience to react in a warm-up. Laughter and applause are encouraged, but not heckling, unless for a very specific moment. Some studios use applause signs to **cue** the audience.*

Confusion and lack of confidence among the actors and crew can be caused by a director who has not organized the rehearsal properly and has ended up shouting through the **talkback.** Therefore, most directors try to rehearse carefully and learn to coax improvements out of the actors and crew. Over-rehearsing can lead to boring, unmotivated performances, while under-rehearsing causes uncertainty and loss of momentum.

Being prepared

As the rehearsal of a scene or a sequence often takes place just before shooting, the actors are fully made up and in costume, and the sets and props are in place. If the director, in the **control room,** spots something wrong with the make-up and costumes, then small changes can usually be made to improve them. Lighting and camera angles can be adjusted, too, but there is only so much that a director can do if the walls, for instance, are the wrong color. Altering the camera exposure cannot change a pale wall into an authentically dark one. Nor can a dark set be made to look realistically light by bleaching it with bright lights. It is important to get these things right when the set is being built.

The director guides the rehearsal from the production control room, where preview monitors show him or her if the planned shots are still effective. Any instructions to the actors, the floor manager, and the lighting and camera crew are made through a talkback.

On the job

A TV director needs to be able to visualize how dialogue and characters will look and sound on television, as well as have a good technical knowledge of filming and a lot of patience. You could first try making your own short videos with some friends. Try to give some shape to the scenes you are creating, even if you are not following a storyline. Many would-be directors go to film school, which can lead them first into directing educational and promotional materials and TV commercials.

Setting the Scene

Some sitcoms are like made-for-TV films, using a lot of outside locations as well as the studio, while others are more like stage productions with an audience. Both types need sets—custom-made rooms in which the "situation" takes place.

Creating a scene

Staging is the process of designing the set and placing scenery and **props** (or properties) in a way that provides an identifiable sense of place and atmosphere without dominating the characters and the dialogue. The set designer always has to bear in mind the positioning of cameras, lighting, and sound equipment. Of utmost importance is safety, in both the materials and structures used and the access to a fire exit. All of these important things are brought together in a floor plan, which the **director** and all the crew work from during filming.

The studio floor is really a large stage divided into different sets and surrounded by a fire safety lane. The skeletons of studio sets are walls made up of flats—lightweight timber frames covered with compressed board, plywood, or canvas. These "flatpacks" are made in various sizes.

Practical scenery—scenery that is functional and makes an appropriate sound when used, such as doors and shutters—is then added to the skeleton. Non-practical scenery—dummy windows, for instance—doesn't work at all. Props are items that can be moved around, such as furniture, ornaments, and potted plants. In sitcoms there can be an element of humor in the props—maybe an outrageous piece of furniture, for instance.

Many pieces of equipment on set have to be hidden. Ceiling tracks hold overhead lighting. Floor lights and those on tripods are kept out of camera shot. Set walls often hide a camera trap—a camouflaged opening that allows a camera to operate secretly. Scaffold catwalks give access to overhead lighting and equipment.

Looking the part

Most sitcoms are domestic or work-based, meaning that costume, make-up, and hair styles just follow current trends. They are really quite ordinary, apart from the occasional garment or hair style that adds to a character's humor. A very precise, pristine suit and tie might seem dull, but when worn by very "straight" comical characters, such as Niles in *Frasier*, with his stiff movements, the starchiness of the costume can become comical. It is the perfect look for his permanent throw-away acting style, where everything is masterfully understated.

Personal props are extra items worn or used by actors, such as umbrellas or a newspaper rolled under the arm. Often, they are an extension of that person's character or role and help to identify it. Action props are essential implements used for a specific action, such as the flashing police siren in the sample sitcom script on page 19. Some are incidental props and just give the actor something to clutch or operate, while others, such as the siren, provide added value to the comedy of the scenario.

Everyone needs some make-up for television, mainly because lighting distorts the color and shape of an actor's face. Sitcom make-up is usually minimal—it just evens out the skin tone and makes the color camera-friendly. Areas of the face that need to look smaller are treated with darker make-up tones, and those that need to stand out are covered with lighter tones.

On the job

The stage hand is the member of the studio crew responsible for putting up scenery and arranging props both in the preproduction and production stages. Stage hands perform mechanical **cues** during shooting, such as crashing something out of camera shot. Stage hands also hold title cards—boards with credits and subtitles—in front of the camera, ready for shooting. To be a stage hand, it helps to have a technical or carpentry qualification. The next step could be work experience in amateur theater and commercials. A stage hand may go on to become a **floor manager.**

The Real Thing

Let's Roll!

Rehearsals are over, and the floor plan and shooting script have established where all the scenery, **props,** crew, and equipment should be placed. The **director** is in the production **control room,** and the actors are in position waiting for their first **cue.**

What is happening on the set?

The actors and crew are in place and waiting for the first shot to be taken. Each sequence is a small bite of the script or action. Each attempt at getting the sequence right is called a **take,** and a **prerecorded** sitcom can go through many takes and many hours before the recording is completed. The end result is smoother than a **live**-filmed sitcom with an audience, which is shot using longer takes, but prerecording is less spontaneous.

The slate shows details of each take: the scene and take numbers, the date, and a clock to show the time. Sometimes this information is written on a board and held in front of a camera for shooting, but it is now mostly produced electronically. The electronic slate gives the actors an automatic countdown to the take so that they can prepare themselves.

*This **sound technician** is holding a long pole, known as a boom, with a microphone at the far end. It allows him to place the mike over the actors without getting in the way of the camera. For large studio sets, the microphone is often suspended from a larger, heavier pole mounted either on a trolley or a tripod.*

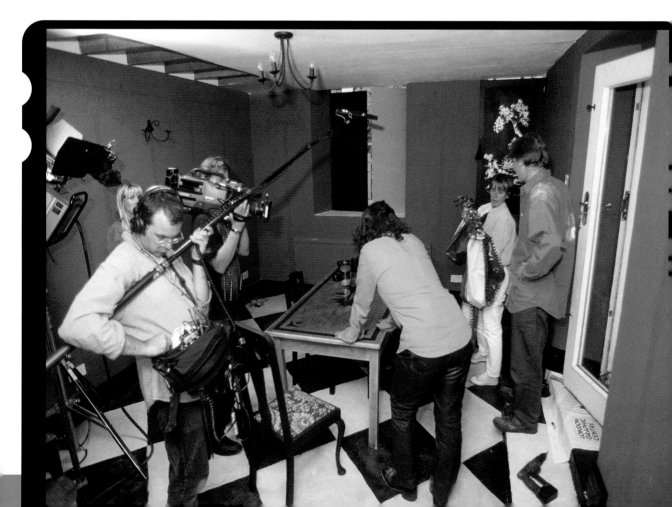

On page 19 we saw that the writer had given a direction for the camera operator. This was an establishing shot—a view of the set as a whole with actors going about their business. Many scenes begin with an establishing shot just to show you the location and who is there. They might then continue with close shots focused on a smaller group of people talking to each other. For these types of shot, the camera usually angles itself to favor one of the characters over another. This is to give the favored character the importance emphasized by the dialogue. Action shots are usually few but meaningful in sitcoms. This is as much due to the restrictions of the set as it is to the **genre** itself.

The next move

Actors and crew operating equipment both need cues to spur them into action. Sometimes the cues are prearranged—a camera might move into position once an actor has sat down or spoken a particular line, for instance. At other times, the **floor manager** will give a hand signal. Foldbacks—acoustics and music played near the set—are often used as cues, as well as being part of the action.

After each take and scene everyone on set is asked to wait while the director views the tape on a monitor in the control room. This means that any corrections to a particular sequence can be done quickly. It also allows for the replacement of props and for any costume or make-up alterations to be made.

Technical tips

These are just a few of the other shots that might be used on a sitcom set:

✿ Detail shot — a sudden shot of something small and very close up, such as the mouthpiece of a telephone receiver, that disrupts the continuity of the main sequence.

✿ Reaction shot — a shot of someone responding to what has just been said or done.

✿ Pickup — this can be any shot that is inserted during the **editing** stage, such as the detail shot above, or it can be a new shot of a character who has just been filmed from a different camera, but who is carrying on dialogue smoothly while the shot changes.

Lights, Camera, Action!

A camera operator, working with the **director** and the lighting crew, is both a technician and an artist, bringing out the drama, humor, and atmosphere of a script and performance. The camera operator's first priority, though, is to shoot a clear picture at the correct angle and from the right distance.

Choosing the camera

Most television programs are filmed using TV or video cameras, rather than movie cameras. The cameras and techniques are basically similar, but TV cameras use videotape, making it easy to rewind and watch immediately. Movie cameras, on the other hand, use film that requires processing and cannot be viewed until this has been done. This means that different **editing** methods are used during the postproduction stage. During shooting, the TV camera operator follows instructions from a set of camera cards that follow the **camera script,** but only give the busy operator what he or she needs to know.

Letting in the light

Before filming begins, the lighting is carefully set up and adjusted to produce the required effect for a particular sequence. One scene may need to be dimly lit, for example, while another should be bright. In the studio, sitcoms are filmed using several cameras, each contributing different shots to the final broadcast. To ensure that all the shots for a particular scene are consistent, the different cameras output to an engineer, who checks that the color and exposure of each is identical.

If a scene is shot on location by a single camera, the camera operator adjusts the camera according to the strength and direction of the lighting so that the videotape does not turn out bleached or blackened when it is **transmitted.** To do this, he or she changes the size of the camera's aperture. The aperture is like the iris of an eye, which lets in more light as it opens and less as it closes. So in a very dimly lit scene, it is opened quite wide, and vice-versa on a brightly lit set.

Lighting it up

The studio needs a flexible lighting system with different intensities and qualities that can be directed to all parts of the set. To this end, some lights are suspended from the ceiling, some are held on tripods, and others are just set on the ground and angled up or down. A simple lighting set-up for a couple of people talking while standing in a room (a typical sitcom scene) could comprise a key light to illuminate the front of the subjects, a backlight to outline their shapes from behind, and fill-ins to dilute the shadows. The first two would shine from ceiling lamps suspended from tracks. The fill-ins could be floor lamps or tripod-mounted lamps positioned at the sides.

Casters and dollies

TV cameras are held on tripods, rolling tripods with casters on the legs, or "dollies," which are wheeled platforms. They can also be mounted on pedestals, which allow great flexibility of movement. The cameras on set are numbered so that if the director or senior camera operator wishes to change the shot, he or she can easily instruct the camera operators how to move through an intercom in the **control room.** The camera operator receives instructions through headphones.

On the job

A camera operator needs to know all the technical aspects of filming, such as the effects of different lighting, filters, and angles on the finished shot, both indoors on set and outdoors on location. He or she must be able to read the camera script, but also be prepared to follow new instructions if a director changes the shot. A camera operator needs to be aware of everything that is going on, especially the movements of actors around him or her. Very importantly, he or she needs to be a good team player.

Television cameras contain thousands of light sensors, or tiny picture cells called **pixels.** *These sensors break up the shape, color, and intensity of the image into patterns that are then translated into electrical signals. These are then changed into radio waves. The waves are sent via a* **transmitter** *to the receiver, your television set, which changes the signals back into pictures (see pages 36 and 40).*

How Does It Sound?

Comedy can be silent—highly comical moments are often very visual—but for most of us, the sitcom would not be as funny without all those wisecracks. So, the **director** has to consider the quality of the sound as well as the picture.

*Members of the sound team receive instructions from the control room through headphones. They make sure that the microphones are in the right positions, which can be difficult on a sitcom set with all the cameras and **props.** Audience microphones are suspended from a track.*

Where is it coming from?

Sound for general television programs comes from many different sources, both **live** and **prerecorded,** but for the sitcom, apart from title and end sequence music and the occasional theme tune that might be associated with a particular character, most sound is direct dialogue and on-set sound effects. These are picked up by different types of microphones and recorded onto the same videotape as the pictures so that picture and sound are synchronized. The sound is also fed into a sound **control room** so that the technicians can adjust it, as we will see on the following two pages.

Microphones can be either mono or stereo. Stereo mikes are really two mono mikes in the same case. If the performers in a sitcom are far apart, one microphone may be used for each of them and then the two sounds **mixed** into stereo. If you watch a sitcom where there are four or five people on the screen at the same time, you will notice that the sound coming from each seems to come from the right place. To achieve this, the **sound technician** uses a mono microphone for each and the sounds are then mixed into the right places. On location, with no complicated sound mixers available, it makes sense to use stereo microphones.

Talking heads

Most microphone heads contain a sensitive **electromagnetic** device to pick up sound waves, which are then changed into a fluctuating electric current. Some microphones are designed to receive sounds from all directions and are used in group and crowd situations or where the background effects are an important part of a scenario. Others only receive sound from certain directions. A ribbon microphone, for instance, picks up sound on a thin, magnetized, metallic strip, and it is good at picking up sounds both in front of it and behind it, but ignores those at the side.

Microphone mistakes

If you have ever tried recording yourself, you will know how difficult it is to avoid getting awful screeching noises and a voice that sounds like a cheese grater. Misdirecting the microphone is one of the worst, but easiest, mistakes to make, and only a lot of experience will ensure that this does not happen too often. A badly-placed microphone leads to jarring distortion of a voice, music, or sound effect. Some microphones are designed to pick up only the voice that you want. The shotgun microphone, for example, only picks up the sound source that it is pointing toward.

The sound technician monitors and adjusts sound level to maintain continuity, especially when a character moves from one part of the set to another. Background noise has to be controlled, although most unwanted noises can be wiped out when the sound is mixed in the control room. If background noises are required, such as waves crashing against a shore, they can be added as special effects, even if the scene is being filmed by the sea. Sound effects ensure quality and continuity, which the natural background noises might not provide. Today, different sounds can be recorded on CDs and then selected by computer. These are known as **digital** effects.

On the job

A sound technician needs a very sharp ear and the ability to work with a script. It is also important to have quick reactions to cope with sudden changes of instruction. Sound technicians need an audio technician's qualification, or certificate, but you could gain experience by recording your school band or a local pop group.

From Camera to Control Room

Viewers see only what is happening on the set. But plenty goes on behind the scenes. Picture and sound have to be monitored and altered constantly to make the perfect program.

Where do all the wires go?

Cables **transmit** pictures and sound from the TV cameras and audio equipment through a wall and into **control rooms,** where the activities on set can be monitored and adjusted. Pictures are routed to monitors in the video control room, while sound is transmitted to the audio control room, where it is fed through to monitor loudspeakers. Here, while shooting is in progress, the **sound technician** balances the outputs from each microphone, making sure that the voice or effect that needs to be prominent stands out as it should.

Control rooms are also where pictures can be **edited** and sounds **mixed** after filming is completed, but before they are put through to the central, or master, control room. In the master control room, everything for programs being produced by that particular studio, or company, is collected and rerouted. This includes outside broadcasts (remotes), such as news reports. From the master control room, these tapes can be made into a master tape or relayed via **transmitters** into your home.

There are many monitors in the control room, each showing shots from a different camera. Once the vision mixer has put together the selected images, they are shown on a main master monitor. TV is usually filmed on videotape, which, unlike film, is never actually physically cut and spliced during the editing process.

The art of editing

The point of the control room is also to put together the best images and sound creatively, manipulating them to keep the plot running, add to the atmosphere of a situation, or enhance the emotions of a character. For visual images, this editing process involves mainly the **director,** technical director, and a technician using a **vision mixer.** The sound supervisor, again under the control of the director and technical director, combines audio material from all sources, both **live** and **prerecorded.** This could include studio microphones, soundtracks from film and video, and CD tracks.

Images are cut and mixed using a vision mixer—a series of buttons that can transform a selection of shots into a meaningful sequence. There are many ways of linking shots. The mix, or dissolve, fades out one shot and fades in another. The two images are superimposed on each other for a short time as the process takes place. In sitcoms, the dissolve is a common way of changing scenes or time, and the fade usually occurs at an average pace. Slow fades can be used to introduce a dream sequence or suggest that something is happening in the past or far future. Fast mixes give a busy feeling, that things are happening in different settings at the same time. These are often used for police series, such as *NYPD Blue*.

A cut, used for high drama and excitement, chops off one shot and switches directly to another. The wipe is where one shot is slowly pushed off screen and another is inserted, moving across the first one. The edge between the two images can be sharp or blurred, and can move quickly or slowly depending on the desired effect.

The soundtrack has to be kept up to speed with the editing of the images. If a scene has many cuts, the director has to make sure that the dialogue, the sound effects, and the music still work with the resulting sequence.

Invisible Waves

Several million people have turned on their television sets just in time to hear the signature tune of their favorite sitcom. It is being broadcast from the studio's master **control room,** via **transmitters,** onto the screen. How do the pictures and sound travel?

Perfect pictures

With **analog** television, sound and pictures are carried from the studio to your television set by radio waves, which can travel very long distances by means of transmitters. Special equipment in the transmitter station changes the pictures and sounds into a form that can travel. A transducer converts them into a varying electrical voltage, or electrical impulse. An oscillation generator converts the electrical power into radio waves, and an amplifier increases the intensity of the waves. The waves are picked up by the receiver in your television set, which reverses the process of the television transmitter, changing the electric impulses back into pictures and sound.

When you turn your television set to a **terrestrial** channel you are really connecting it to a transmitter. This in turn links back to the television station. Each of these three pieces of equipment uses **antennae,** or aerials, to "catch" the radio waves that carry the pictures and sound of the program. Your television set has to be tuned so that it will receive the correct **frequency** of radio waves for a particular channel. But what are frequencies, and what are waves?

On the right wavelength

Radio waves pulsate with different wavelengths and for different distances. They are used not only for television, but also for radio, telephone, radar, navigational systems, and space communication. Each type of wave travels with a kind of pulse—moving at a certain number of cycles every second. This is its frequency. The shortest waves have the most cycles per second, which means they have the highest frequency. The longest waves have the least cycles per second, or the lowest frequency. The cycles per second are known as hertz and are named after the early German radio scientist, Heinrich Hertz.

Television is transmitted on very high, short frequencies. Two of the highest frequencies are megahertz (MHz), with a wave rate of a million cycles per second, and gigahertz (GHz), with a billion cycles per second. Radio waves can have several GHz! These really high frequencies are called VHF (very high frequency), UHF (ultra-high frequency), and SHF (super-high frequency). The waves are incredibly short and difficult to transmit terrestrially without many transmitting stations to "string" them together.

Transmitting the waves

Radios are often marked with the letters AM and FM, which stand for **Amplitude Modulation** and **Frequency Modulation.** These are also used for television **transmission** and are types of varied, or modulated, waves. Modulation allows a television set to receive all the different notes and tones of speech, music, and sound effects, and the lightness and darkness of the picture. FM waves are usually carried at VHF—very high frequency—which means that they are short and do not travel as far as AM, which is often carried at very low frequencies. To compensate for this, antennae or aerials transmitting FM often have to be extremely tall. Placing tall antennae can be very impractical, so FM stations are often more successfully broadcast through telephone wires or special cables.

These are television transmitters. There is a limited amount of space on the planet for the clear transmission of signals, so most countries allocate a certain number of **wavebands** *for each television station. The transmission of analog signals requires wide wavebands. If TV signals are transmitted outside their allotted waveband they can interfere with other channels.*

New Ways for Waves

Analog terrestrial television, which we have just explored, is still the most widely-received television throughout the world, but satellite, cable, and **digital** television are giving many people access to an increasing number of television stations. Cable and digital TV have also raised the quality of **transmission.**

Making space

As we have seen, there is a limited amount of space for signals on earth. Since the 1960s, scientists have been trying to find ways of increasing transmission capacity, to enable the broadcast of more electronic mass communication signals and reach a wider audience.

A satellite is an unmanned spacecraft that orbits along a known path around our planet, making it easy to track and reliable to use for bouncing signals—usually! Different types and makes of satellites have varying transmission capabilities. Most modern communications satellites handle telephone, radio, and television signals, serving several TV and radio stations and hundreds of thousands of phone calls at once.

Satellite

Satellite television was the first development along these lines, initially allowing different studios to transmit to each other. It uses ground transmission stations, just like terrestrial TV, but instead of using a string of **transmitters** to broadcast programs over a long distance, waves emitted from ground stations reach up into space, where they bounce off a satellite and back down again. A satellite dish is turned to the correct angle to capture the waves. The late 1970s saw the beginning of satellite transmission in people's homes.

Cable

Cable television receives a lot of channels from satellite stations, but transmits them underground through copper-wire or optical-fiber cables (see picture) to individual homes. Each cable television company runs cables from its central control unit, called a headend. The headend is attached to a huge satellite dish that receives several stations.

The digital age

Digital television can be carried by terrestrial transmitter, satellite, and cable. It is the digital signals themselves that are different. They are regular streams of electrical pulses, all the same size. The lack of variation means that they do not need a wide transmission band, unlike analog signals. Many digital stations can fit into the same wave space needed by just one analog station.

Digital transmission differs in another way, too. The sound and light waves of a television program are translated into a binary code, just like a computer program. The code cannot be altered by static or any other type of electrical interference. This, plus the steady electrical pulse itself, makes the transmission smoother and easier to control.

Each optical fiber in the bundle is made up of two very long, thin strands of glass, one wrapped around the other. When a light beam is shone into one end of the fiber, it travels along the inner strand, bouncing at an angle where the inner and outer strands meet. The outer glass tube stops the light from escaping. Because the light bounces at an angle as it goes, it can shoot around bends. It can also travel a very long way.

Technical tips

In digital transmission, the code carrying a TV program's pictures and sound reaches your television set, where a special digital box or device translates the code back into pictures and sound. Most wealthy countries—that is about a fifth of the world—now have an Integrated Services Digital Network (ISDN) that allows television, radio, telephone, and computer data to be transmitted along the same line.

Light Fantastic

Your television picture is mostly **transmitted** by a system not much different from an ordinary radio broadcasting station. The sound equipment is like that used in **FM** radio broadcasting, and the sound signal is sometimes broadcast from its own unit, separate from the pictures. There are, however, several things that make television different.

Scanning

Every moving image has to be read by the camera, like reading pages of text in a book. Just as individual words on the page are put together to make sense, so a picture is broken up into tiny pieces by the television camera and then reconstructed on the television screen. The device used to break up the image and put the pieces back together again is the scanner. The scanner's eye—a beam of electrons—moves across the image picked up by the camera's thousands of picture cells, or **pixels.** As it does so, it responds to the amount of light given out by each pixel by generating an electrical signal proportionate to the brightness. Of course, this all happens in a split second. In fact, many whole pictures can be scanned within a single second. In a **live** broadcast, a **transmitter** scanner in a TV camera is in turn read by the television scanner in a TV set in exact synchronization, translating the electrical signals back into pixels. This is how you see your picture.

The magic box

Television transmission needs special circuits for scanning pictures and devices for monitoring the signals from the television camera. When the signals reach the television set, they run through a circuit made of **transistors** and integrated circuits (microchips). These instruct the signals to change into patterns of light made up of as many as a million tiny colored pixels. Bundles of three colors of light are used—red, green, and blue—from which all the other colors are made. When blended together, the resulting colors are different from the mixed colors in your paintbox. In any case, blending is not really what happens. The color television screen is built to deceive the eye; it is actually the eye that blends the colors.

The colored pixels are laid out in a pattern. When an image is transmitted onto the screen, different intensities of light shine on the pixels that make the shapes in the picture. For instance, if the image is of a yellow sandy desert, then the red and green pixels will be activated to a certain intensity, which gives the correct hue. This idea is not new. The nineteenth-century French artist Georges Seurat created paintings made entirely of stippled dots of different colors. A patch of green, for instance, was made up of many separate dots of blue and yellow, and close up that is all you can see. It is only when you stand back from the picture that you see green.

On the job

An electronics design engineer needs to be good at science, especially physics, mathematics, and information technology. Most electronics design engineers have a college degree. Their work may involve helping to develop the next generation of television sets or transmission techniques, such as plasma screens.

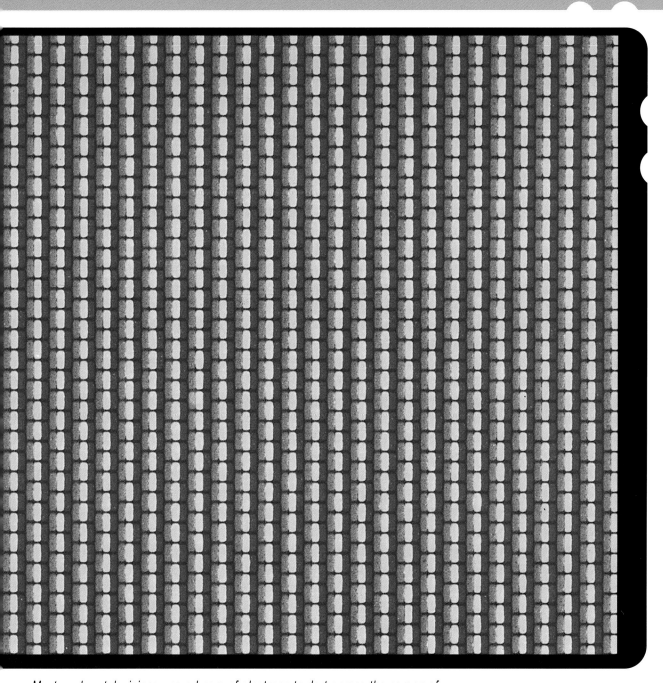

Most modern televisions use a beam of electrons to dart across the screen of tubes that receive the picture signals. The tubes hold thousands of tiny pixels, like the ones you see above. Pixels are scanned extremely quickly, which gives a moving picture. The television screen also has a black-and-white receiver, which ignores the instructions for color and color intensity so that it can produce black, white, and gray tones.

Technical tips

In a television camera, the scanner's electron beam moves rapidly backward and forward as it scans the image. It scans the image only as it goes forward. As it goes backward to the beginning of the next line, the beam's current shuts off.

The End of the Show

Taking a Break

So technology has brought the sitcom to your screen, but the show is not all you will see while watching. Commercial breaks and news items can precede, interrupt, or follow the sitcom. Occasionally, sudden bulletins might flash on the screen.

*In the studio **control room**, the sitcom show, advertisements, news bulletins, trails, and links are all cued in from different studios, **prerecorded** tapes, and outside broadcasts. Outside broadcasts are now **transmitted** to the studio mostly by satellite.*

What grabs you?

Commercials help to pay for the sitcom and every other program on commercial television. They can also be informative and entertaining, promoting all kinds of products and services, from local goods to international brand names. Commercial slots are also sold to organizations, charities, religious groups, and political parties. The sitcom itself is advertised on television through trails or promos—enticing sequences isolated from the episode and promoted by an enthusiastic voice-over.

A television station's head of programming will want to fill advertising slots with commercials that are in some way relevant to the program being interrupted, or the kind of people who would be watching the program. Like advertisers, the programmer has to know the profile of the viewer. He or she uses many of the techniques employed by the product manufacturers and advertising agencies themselves to learn more about the viewers.

A commercial campaign begins with finding out what will attract people to buy a product, use a service, or listen to a politician. From these narrowed-down opinions and ideas, storyboards are made. Storyboards are detailed sketches of ideas for a television commercial, usually with a punchy slogan or end-line.

Styles of commercial vary tremendously, from slick and sophisticated to simple and silly. Some are mini-series, featuring a long-running story in which the same actors develop their characters over a single campaign, or even over a number of years, for the same product.

Perfect presentation

Continuity announcers often lead the viewer into the sitcom, and at the same time introduce trails for other programs. Their links provide a smooth transition between the slots and make the viewer aware of any changes in the schedule. You will not normally see the continuity announcer, as they are usually employed for their voice, which should be soothing and calm and keep the viewer tuned to the station. Sometimes, at the end of a news bulletin, a newscaster is used to deliver the same information as the continuity announcer. If the bulletin is sudden, then the newscaster will return the audience back to the program they were watching, but the news presenter might be seen, and not just heard.

This is the news

When you watch someone reading the news, all you will see is a desk, papers, and the newscaster him or herself, with tiny intercom earphones behind the ears. You will also see a screen behind the presenter, which brings up any image chosen from monitors positioned in front of him or her, but out of sight for us. The workings of the news studio are kept out of sight. News items are carefully timed, but we do not see the clock, **cue**-light, and **floor manager** all helping the newscaster to keep to the schedule. The newscaster mostly reads from a prompter, which is a monitor with a narrow, scrolled script in a large, clear font.

The news presenter has to time news items and interviews to the second. He or she also has to lead into other presenters, such as those specializing in weather or sports. News presenters have to be ready to react to news flashes brought to them over the intercom.

The Verdict and Future Trends

Sitcoms attract some of the highest **ratings** of all TV entertainment. That is why so much time and money are spent on the best of them. But, how are they rewarded, what is their future, and what lies ahead for television as a whole?

Looking ahead

Sitcoms are reviewed in entertainment magazines, media columns of newspapers and, increasingly, TV review programs. The verdict on any program often depends on the target group of a particular critic and publication. Not many broadsheet newspapers would even bother to make comment on a teen sitcom, and probably few young people would care about their opinion! The future of the sitcom perhaps lies in **producers'** attitudes toward their viewers—with the increasing number of television channels, perhaps they won't be able to take the audience for granted and will have to produce shows of higher quality. However, have more TV stations given more choice, or just more of the same thing? While they do allow local and minority broadcasting, they have also encouraged "lazy" television, with lots of reruns, especially of sitcoms.

In technical terms, the future for television is already here. Satellite and cable **transmission** have both made television more accessible and varied. Pay-per-view stations allow people to see more programs of their choice. Interactive TV, such as video games and shopping channels, has broadened TV's role, while vidicon transmission, used for closed-circuit television, has captured pictures of Earth from space. The next step is the expansion of **digital** and Internet television.

Was it decent, honest, and fair?

With an increase in the number of TV sets per household, viewing has changed from a family entertainment to a solitary pursuit. This has led to greater anxiety and scrutiny over the suitability of programs for young people, with regard to violence, bad language, sick humor, horror, or sexual innuendo that they may contain. Independent, statutory, and industry-led organizations, such as the U.S. Christian Family Monitor group, examine the content of TV programs. In the U.S., laws protecting freedom of speech make it difficult to enforce many complaints. In other countries, however, complaints are often upheld.

Technical tips

✧ Digital TV has been marketed as the future of television, but energy conservationists have warned that it uses up a lot of power. It is thought that by 2010, a country the size of the U.K. will be burning seven percent more fossil fuels because of the "thirsty" digital TV.

✧ The digital loop enables pay-per-view customers to call a TV company and ask for a particular film to be transmitted on their TV screen. This service will surely extend to other types of programs in the near future.

✧ High Density Television (HDTV) has improved picture quality by doubling the number of lines per screen.

*The future of the sitcom looks bright. TV awards ceremonies, such as the Emmy Awards, consistently reward sitcom actors, writers, and **directors.** The sitcom's international appeal is likely to continue as well. In May 2000, Interactive TV Provider in the U.K. announced its winners in a poll of top British TV characters of all time—all three were from sitcoms.*

On the job

Television reviewers need very good writing skills and a passion for the small screen. They also need to understand what other people like to watch, and why they watch it, so that they know what could appeal to others even if it is not to their own taste. You could start your career by reviewing programs for your school or community newspaper. Keep clippings of your reviews so that you can show them to your local newspaper. They may give you a column! Many reviewers have media degrees.

Glossary

Amplitude Modulation (AM)   type of modulated (varied) signal along which sound waves are transmitted

analog   sound and pictures that are translated into radio waves by a TV station's transmitter, and then translated back to sound and pictures inside the television set

antenna   (or aerial) a structure for sending out and receiving sound and picture signals

camera script   script with camera instructions marked on it for the camera crew to follow

casting   finding the actors for all the parts played in a sitcom

closure   episode of a series with an ending to the storyline—it does not carry over to the next episode

commission   when a producer chooses a particular writer to write a sitcom

control room   room with television monitors in which editing and mixing take place and from which a director can instruct the floor manager and crew

cue   a signal to actors and the production team to begin talking, shooting, recording, and so on

culture-specific   relating to a particular group of people who share the same culture. In terms of televising sitcoms, targeting this group by using humor that it can instantly recognize.

digital   radio waves that are converted into a computerized form for transmission, making them more stable and enabling more to be transmitted at one time

director   person who interprets the script, works with the set designer to create the visual image of the sitcom, and directs the style and movement of the actors

dub   dialogue that is recorded in a different language from the original; also, recorded sound that is copied onto a different tape, or sound added to others on a tape

edit   to choose, put together, and manipulate shots and sequences on the videotape or film

electromagnetic   made of a piece of magnetized metal and used to pick up sound waves

executive producer   person in overall control of the budget and oversight of a sitcom, from preproduction to postproduction

floor manager (**FM**)   supervisor who makes sure that everything runs smoothly on set or in the studio; he or she also controls a live TV audience

format   way a particular type of program is arranged

frequency   pulse of a radio wave moving at a certain number of cycles per second

Frequency Modulation (FM)   type of modulated (varied) signal along which sound and picture are carried

genre   particular type or style of program, such as sitcom, documentary, or game show

inflection   variation of the voice; the way pitch moves up and down as we speak

language-specific   referring to a particular language. In terms of televising sitcoms, creating humor using specific elements of a particular language, such as puns.

live   a program transmitted immediately to its audience

mix   different sounds, such as special effects and music, that are blended and put together on one tape

network   system of television stations that are linked in order to broadcast the same programs

pixel   tiny picture cell which, together with thousands of others that make the television screen, is lit to create the picture

prerecorded   a program recorded and edited before it is transmitted

prime time   evening hours between about 7:00 P.M. and 10:00 P.M., when the most people watch television

producer   person who controls the running of the sitcom from preproduction to postproduction stages. This person works under the executive producer.

prop   a movable item, such as a chair or coffee pot, used to create the right environment on set

ratings   calculation of the size of the audience for each television program

serial   drama divided into episodes—each episode tells a different part of the story and often ends with a cliffhanger

slapstick   humor based on practical jokes or boisterous play-acting

sound technician   member of the technical crew who places and operates the microphones, balances the output, and checks sound levels

stereotype   a fixed, and often not positive, image of a person or group of people

take   a shot or sequence, or different version of that shot or sequence

talkback   two-way radio system from a studio control room to a recording studio or a set, often used to feed instructions from the director to the floor manager

terrestrial   transmitting system that sends signals via transmitters on Earth, not by satellite

transistor   device used in microphones, radios, and other sound equipment to control the electric current running through it

transmit, transmission   1) to broadcast a program 2) another word for the program that is broadcast

transmitter   equipment that produces, modulates, and sends out radio signals

vision mixer   machine that puts together images brought to the control room by the different cameras; the person who operates the vision mixer machine

waveband   band of wavelengths along which a program's radio waves are sent

Index

actors 18, 20–23, 24, 25, 28, 29
AM and FM 37
analog terrestrial TV 15, 36, 38
audiences 23, 24
awards 5, 45

boom 28

cable television 15, 39, 44
camera operators 24, 29, 30, 31
camera script 18, 24, 30
cameras 30
canned laughter 23
casting directors 18, 20
censorship 6, 7
character comedies 17
characterization 10, 12
commercials 42–43
continuity announcers 43
control rooms 25, 28, 30, 33, 34–35, 42
costumes 15, 25, 27
creative teams 9
cues 18, 27, 28, 29
culture-specific humor 8, 13

digital television 5, 39, 44
directors 10, 15, 17, 18, 20, 24, 25, 26, 28, 29, 32, 35
dubbing and subtitling 7, 13, 23

editing 30, 34, 35
electronics design engineers 40
executive producers 14, 16

financing TV programs 14, 15
floor managers (FMs) 18, 24, 25, 27, 29
foldbacks 29
frequencies 36

game shows 7

High Density Television (HDTV) 44

independent commercial companies 7
Integrated Services Digital Network (ISDN) 39
interactive television 44
Internet television 6, 44
invention of television 5

lighting 4, 18, 25, 26, 30
live production 16, 24, 28, 33, 35, 40

make-up 15, 25, 27
method acting 20, 21
microphones 28, 32, 33
mixing 33, 34, 35
music 33

network television companies 6
news reports 34, 43

pay-per-view television 44
pixels 31, 40, 41,
prerecording 16, 24, 28, 33, 35, 42
prime time 13, 15
producers 9, 10, 14, 15, 16, 17, 44
production costs 15
profits 15
props 4, 24, 26, 27

radio waves 36
ratings 7, 9, 14, 15, 16, 20, 44
regulation 7
rehearsals 24–25
rehearse-record technique 24
reviewers 44, 45

satellite television 6, 15, 38, 44
scanner 40, 41
scenery 26
script-readers 10, 16
serial format 9
set designers 26
sets 4, 9, 15, 25, 26

sitcom (situation comedy)
  actors 20–23, 24, 25, 28, 29
  age grouping 11, 16
  characterization and plot 9, 10
  format 9, 23
  preproduction phase 16
  production costs 15
  rehearsals and shooting 24–33
  reviews and awards 44, 45
  scheduling 16
  scripts 18–19
  titles 17
slapstick humor 8, 13
sound quality 32–33
sound technicians 28, 32, 33, 34, 35
soundtrack 35
stage hands 27
staging 26
stereotypes 12
studios 26

takes 21, 24, 28, 29
talkback 25
television ownership 4
title cards 27
transmitters and receivers 34, 36, 37, 39, 40

vision mixer 34–35

wavebands 7, 37
writers 9, 10, 15, 18–19